AWFUL
AVALANCHES

Jane Katirgis and Michele Ingber Drohan

Enslow Publishing
101 W. 23rd Street
Suite 240
New York, NY 10011
USA

enslow.com

WORDS TO KNOW

concrete—A hard, strong building material made by mixing cement with water, rocks, and gravel.

crystals—Particles that form when certain substances become solid, such as water becoming ice.

friction—The rubbing of one thing against another.

gravity—A natural force that causes objects to be attracted to each other.

oxygen—A colorless gas that makes up part of the air we breathe.

particle—A small piece of something.

predict—To think and say something is going to happen before it happens.

snowpack—The layers of snow that have built up on a slope.

threaten—To show the possibility of causing harm.

vapor—The gas that is formed when a liquid heats up and evaporates.

Contents

When groups of ice crystals get heavy enough, they fall as snow.

1

THE SCIENCE OF SNOW

Snow is made of many different ice **crystals**. Ice crystals form when water **vapor** in the air freezes. These crystals come together around a dust **particle**. As more crystals come together, the clump gets heavy. When it grows heavy enough, the group of crystals falls from the sky. This group of ice crystals is called a snowflake. As a snowflake falls, it changes shape. That is why no two snowflakes are the same.

This magnified view shows the ice crystal structure of a snowflake.

SNOWFLAKE SHAPES

The shape of each snowflake is very important. Some shapes make the snow strong, but others make the snow weak. Strong snow stays together well. Weak snow shifts around. A lot of weak snow may be an avalanche in the making.

2

AVALANCHE AHEAD!

What exactly is an avalanche? An avalanche is a big pile of snow that slides down a mountain slope. When the snow can no longer stick together, **gravity** pulls it down. Two things are needed to start an avalanche. One is a slope covered with snow. The other is a trigger, or something that makes the snow move. An avalanche trigger can be wind, a skier, or even the sound of someone's voice.

A skier in action may trigger an avalanche.

To understand the possible danger of an avalanche, we must first look at the different layers of snow on the slope.

SNOW LAYERS

As snow falls and hits the ground, many layers build on top of one another. This makes a **snowpack**. We know that snowflakes change as they fall. The snow continues to change even after it hits the ground. Snow can change because of the sun, the wind, or the temperature. When ice crystals are shaped in a way that makes it hard for the snow to stick together, a weak layer of snow is formed in the snowpack. A weak layer of snow will slide easily. The type of avalanche that happens depends on where this weak layer is found.

A weak layer of snow in a snowpack can slide easily. It can cause an avalanche.

MOUNT EVEREST'S MONSTER AVALANCHE

In April 2014, Mount Everest guides, called Sherpas, were bravely climbing frozen trails. The Sherpas were setting up ropes and carrying supplies. Later, climbers from all over the world would use the trails and supplies. They would try to reach the top of the tallest mountain on earth. Nineteen thousand feet (5,791 m) in the air, disaster struck.

A large ice block broke apart and caused an avalanche. Some men jumped behind chunks of ice to stay safe. Others survived because they were tied to climbing ropes. Twenty-five men were buried in the snow. Tragically, sixteen of those men died.

This candlelight ceremony took place to honor the sixteen Sherpas who died in the avalanche.

3

TYPES OF AVALANCHES

Sluff avalanches and slab avalanches are the two main types of avalanches.

SLUFF AVALANCHE

A sluff avalanche happens when a weak layer of snow is on the top of a snowpack. Sluffs are not very dangerous because they don't carry lots of snow. The snow they do carry is light like powder. Sluffs occur most often after a big snowstorm. New snow piles on top of snow that is wet or icy. This smooth surface helps the new snow slide down easily.

A sluff avalanche carries light, powdery snow.

As the snow slides, it gathers more snow with it and spreads out in the shape of a big triangle.

SLAB AVALANCHE

Another type of avalanche is called a slab avalanche. Slab avalanches can be much more dangerous than sluffs. This is because the weak layer of

SLAB AVALANCHE IN COLORADO

It was the morning of April 20, 2013. A group of six people set out in an area called Loveland Pass. Suddenly, they felt a thud and heard a loud *whumpf*! Uphill, a deep slab started to slide.

All six people ran toward a small group of trees, but the large avalanche covered them. Five were completely buried. The one survivor was buried with his arm free above the snow. He was able to yell for help. He was rescued four hours later.

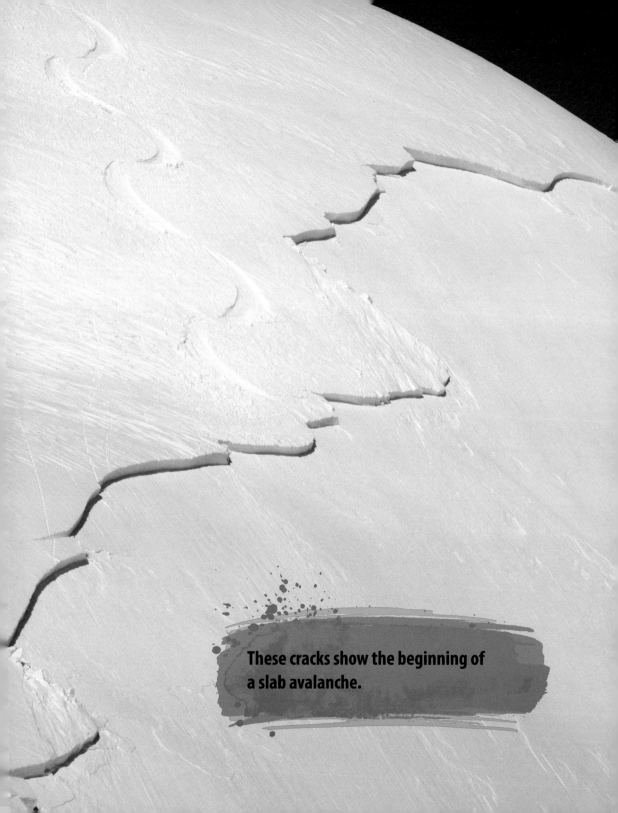

These cracks show the beginning of a slab avalanche.

These cars were no match for an avalanche in Utah.

snow that causes the avalanche is buried deep in the snowpack. When it slides down the slope, all the snow on top of it slides with it. The snow on top is called a slab. It is strong and hard. Slab avalanches carry huge amounts of snow and can move as fast as 200 miles (322 km) per hour! They are so powerful that they take trees and rocks with them down the slope. As the slab rushes down, it heats up from the **friction** and some of the snow melts. When it stops, the snow freezes again and becomes as hard as **concrete**.

4

AVALANCHE SAFETY

Millions of avalanches happen each year all over the world. People are not in danger unless they are in the way. When people ski or hike in an avalanche area, they are in danger. That is why many ski resorts do avalanche control. Experts at ski resorts create avalanches on purpose by shooting at snowpacks with guns. This removes weak snow and frees the slopes of avalanches, which makes them safe. This is done at night or in the morning when nobody can get hurt.

SNOW PROFILE

Date

Order

Time

Incline

Elevation

Pen. of Foot

This man is checking a ski area's avalanche conditions.

Some people ski or hike in places where avalanches are not controlled. Because of this, thousands of people die each year in avalanches that they cause.

AVALANCHE RESCUES

Sometimes a person can be buried under an avalanche. It is very important to find the person fast. This is because there is very little **oxygen** for that person to breathe under the snow. After about twenty minutes, the oxygen usually runs out. Without oxygen, a person will die.

INVENTION TO SAVE LIVES

In 1968, Dr. John Lawton invented a beeper to help find buried avalanche victims. If someone is in an area where an avalanche might happen, he or she wears the beeper. If that person gets buried, the beeper sends out a signal so others can find him or her. Then they can dig the avalanche victim out of the snow.

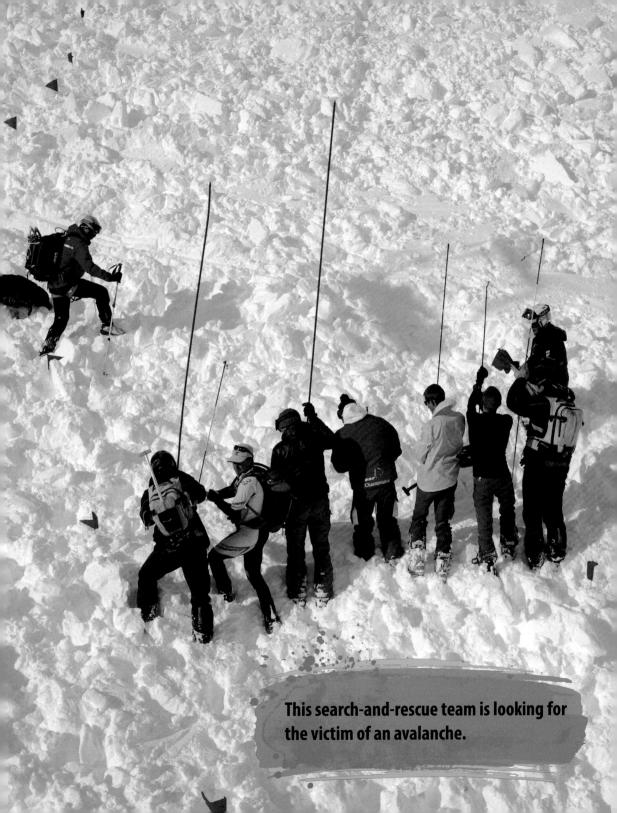

This search-and-rescue team is looking for the victim of an avalanche.

5

DOGS TO THE RESCUE

Avalanche rescue teams know that a victim may not have an avalanche beeper. So rescue teams use dogs to help find victims and dig them out of the snow. Many ski resorts have avalanche dog programs that train dogs to find victims. This is done by teaching the dogs to find objects buried in the snow. A trainer will hide something with a human scent on it then use commands such as "Search!" or "Find 'em!" to tell the dogs to go to

This rescue dog is being trained by its handler to find avalanche victims.

work. The dogs learn to work fast. The trainers know that the faster the dogs work, the better chance there is of saving a life.

AVALANCHE IN ICELAND

Sometimes an avalanche **threatens** an entire town or city. This happened in Flateyri, Iceland, in October 1995. After a week of heavy snowfall, an avalanche warning was sent out. Flateyri has a long history of avalanches. The people there thought they knew which parts of town were safe. People in the dangerous areas moved to safer places in town. However, the avalanche was bigger than anyone in the town had ever seen. It reached farther than any avalanche had before. By the next morning, 250,000 tons (226,796 metric tons) of snow covered Flateyri. Twenty people had been killed, and many homes were lost.

Rescue workers faced the effects of the biggest avalanche that Flateyri, Iceland, had ever seen.

6

AVALANCHE PROTECTION IN THE FUTURE

Avalanche experts do tests to study snowpacks very closely. They look for the weak layers of snow across a whole mountain range. Experts hope to understand how and why the snowpack changes. This could help them **predict** when and where an avalanche may strike. It may also tell them what path the avalanche could take. Until avalanches can be predicted, towns like Flateyri must find ways to protect themselves. The people of Flateyri have built a 60-foot-high (18 m) wall that blocks avalanches and keeps people safe.

Experts study snow to help them predict avalanches.

LEARN MORE

Books

Green, Sara. *Snow Search Dogs*. New York: Scholastic Library Publishing, 2013.

Hynes, Margaret. *Extreme Weather*. New York: Kingfisher, 2013.

Merrick, Patrick. *Avalanches*. North Mankato, Minn.: The Child's World, 2015.

Web Sites

education.nationalgeographic.com/education/media/avalanches-101
Fast facts, quizzes, vocabulary, and video about avalanches.

snowcrystals.com
Photos, snow activities, and the science of snow crystals.

INDEX

Published in 2016 by Enslow Publishing, LLC.
101 W. 23rd Street, Suite 240, New York, NY 10011

Library of Congress Cataloging-in-Publication Data
Katirgis, Jane, author.
 Awful avalanches / Jane Katirgis and Michele Ingber Drohan.
    pages cm. —(Earth's natural disasters)
 Summary: "Discusses the science behind avalanches and what to do to stay safe from them"— Provided by publisher.
 Audience: Ages 8+
 Audience: Grades 4 to 6
 Includes bibliographical references and index.
 ISBN 978-0-7660-6791-2 (library binding)
 ISBN 978-0-7660-6789-9 (pbk.)
 ISBN 978-0-7660-6790-5 (6-pack)
 1. Avalanches—Juvenile literature. 2. Avalanches—Control—Juvenile literature. I. Drohan, Michele Ingber, author. II. Title.
 QC929.A8K38 2016
 551.57'848—dc23
                         2015009963

Printed in the United States of America

Photo Credits: ©AP Images, p. 27; Bob Winset/Photolibrary/Getty Images, p. 9; Cylonphoto/Shutterstock.com, p. 25; EpicStockMedia/Shutterstock.com (chapter openers and back matter backgrounds); Ivan Chudakov/Shutterstock.com, p. 1; James Balog/The Image Bank/Getty Images, p. 18; Jamie Farrant/Digital Vision Vectors (caption boxes); Kenneth Libbrecht/Visuals Unlimited/Getty Images, p. 6; Marco Maccarini/E+/Getty Images, p. 15; Niranjan Shrestha/©AP Images, p. 13; Peter Gudella/Shutterstock.com, p. 23; Photo Researchers/Science Source/Getty Images, p. 11; Rich Wheater/All Canada Photos/Getty Images, p. 21; Sunny Forest/Shutterstock.com, p. 4; Topher Donahue/Aurora/Getty Images; p. 17; traffic_analyzer/Digital Vision Vectors/Getty Images (page folios); Yvette Cardozo/Photolibrary/Getty Images, p. 29.

Cover Credits: Ivan Chudakov/Shutterstock.com (skier); EpicStockMedia/Shutterstock.com (background); traffic_analyzer/Digital Vision Vectors/Getty Images (series icon).